Another Paws

for a moment with God

Devotions
Best Enjoyed in the Company of a Cat

Inspired
by Faith

Another Paws for a moment with God
©Product Concept Mfg., Inc.

Another Paws for a moment with God
ISBN 978-0-9848369-9-4

Published by Product Concept Mfg., Inc.
2175 N. Academy Circle #200, Colorado Springs, CO 80909

©2012 Product Concept Mfg., Inc. All rights reserved.

Written and Compiled by Patricia Mitchell
in association with Product Concept Mfg., Inc.

All scripture quotations are from the King James version
of the Bible unless otherwise noted.

Scriptures taken from the Holy Bible,
New International Version®, NIV®.
Copyright © 1973, 1978, 1984 by Biblica, Inc.™
Used by permission of Zondervan.
All rights reserved worldwide.
www.zondervan.com

Sayings not having a credit listed are contributed by writers
for Product Concept Mfg., Inc. or in a rare case,
the author is unknown.

Another Paws

for a moment with God

*W*ho could imagine a world without our feline friends? They tickle our fancy, warm the heart, and make us laugh out loud. Their comical antics and whimsical ways keep us well entertained, and their gentle affection and quiet companionship fill our home with purrrfect love.

This second book in the Paws series provides devotional readings inspired by cats… some humorous, some serious, but each one food for thought. For your personal reflection, classic quotations follow each reading… words of ageless wisdom that speak to the concerns and questions you face in your life today.

We invite you to snuggle up with the special cat who purrs under your roof… or the one cherished within your heart… and let these words bless you with spiritual rest and relaxation, support and encouragement.

All cats love a cushioned couch.
~*Theocritus*

After breakfast and a little time

to look out the window,

a cat is happy to find a quiet nook

for her morning's nap.

When we take pleasure

in life's simple blessings,

there's something to

please us every day.

Happiness Today

Sometimes we spend so much time thinking about what would bring us happiness that we forget about what does. That is, the things around us every day that we enjoy. Usually, they're things as simple as relaxing on a quiet evening, or chatting with a friend…taking a brisk walk, or watching clouds drift by overhead… and stroking a cat's soft coat, feeling the vibration of her rumbling purr.

Not one of us knows the good things God has in mind for us in the future, but we do know all the blessings He has showered on us today. To discover them, give thanks for them, and take pleasure in them is to find happiness right where we are, every day.

Dear God, thank You for the gift of today
and the many blessings in it.
Amen

What a wonderful life I've had!
I only wish I'd realized it sooner.
Colette

True happiness is to understand
our duties toward God and man; to enjoy the
present, without being anxious about the future;
not to amuse ourselves with hopes and fears,
but to rest satisfied with what we have.
Seneca

Happy is the man that findeth wisdom,
and the man that getteth understanding.
Proverbs 3:13

Pleasure is spread through the earth
in stray gifts to be claimed by whoever shall find.
William Wordsworth

This is the day which the LORD hath made;
we will rejoice and be glad in it.
Psalm 118:24

Earth's crammed with heaven.
Elizabeth Barrett Browning

If you want to be happy, be.
Leo Tolstoy

No path is wholly rough;
look for the places that are smooth and clear.
Ella Wheeler Wilcox

Whoever possesses God is happy.
Augustine

The ideal of calm exists in a sitting cat.
~Jules Renard

In the middle of play,

a cat suddenly stops running and

jumping, and poses completely

still while excitement whirls

around her. When there's a lot

going on in our life, stress is a

sure signal that we need

to take some time out.

No Stress Zone

Stress is bad! It causes tension and irritability, and if left unchecked, can bring on emotional and physical illness.

Stress is good! It's a warning. Stress tells us in no uncertain terms that something isn't right... something needs to change.

That "something" might be a situation demanding a fresh perspective, or a problem calling for a constructive solution. The source of our stress might rest with unchangeable circumstances, signaling our need to find a positive response... a change in thinking, action, or attitude.

Stress is bad or good, depending on what we do with it. We keep it "good" when we answer it by stepping back, taking a clear-eyed look at what's going on in our life, and making changes for the better.

Dear God, help me find ways to
lessen the stress in my life.
Amen

Worry often gives a small thing a big shadow.
Proverb

One must not hope to be more than one can be.
Nicolas de Chamfort

Every morning I spend fifteen minutes
filling my mind full of God, and so there's no
room left for worry thoughts.
Howard Chandler Christy

Cast thy burden upon the LORD,
and he shall sustain thee.
Psalm 55:22

Let us accept truth,
even when it surprises us and alters our views.
George Sand

I know God will not give me anything I can't
handle. I just wish that He didn't trust me so much.
Mother Teresa

Drag your thoughts away from your troubles...
by the ears, by the heels,
or any other way you can manage it.
Mark Twain

Take rest;
a field that has rested gives a bountiful crop.
Ovid

I am convinced that there are times in everybody's
experience when there is so much to be done, that
the only way to do it is to sit down and do nothing.
Fanny Fern

A cat, I am sure, could walk on a cloud
without coming through.
~Jules Verne

The cat allows herself time

to sit and weave private dreams

of distant worlds and faraway

things. She has much to show

us about the gift of imagination...

of dreams...of taking time to

skip on downy clouds.

Wish upon a Star

If you were granted one wish, what would it be? When you were a child, you might have shouted out something like, "Adventurer!" or "Astronaut!" or "Hero!" But what would you wish for now?

As adults, we wish for other things—for good relationships, financial security, success at what we do—but we rarely share our dreams with other people. We're afraid we'll sound silly, and so our dearest desire remains tucked away deep in the heart. Yet if we were to examine it carefully, we'd find within our wish something lying within our reach … something we could start making happen.

In every wishful heart, there's something that could become reality.

Dear God, show me Your divine will within
my fondest hopes and dreams.
Amen

Dream lofty dreams, and as you dream, so shall you become. Your vision is the promise of what you shall at last unveil.
John Ruskin

Ask, and it shall be given you; seek, and ye shall find; knock, and it shall be opened unto you.
Matthew 7:7

A healthful hunger for a great idea is the beauty and blessedness of life.
Jean Ingelow

He who removes a mountain begins by carrying away small stones.
Proverb

Start by doing what's necessary, then what's possible, and suddenly you are doing the impossible.
Francis of Assisi

No first step can be really great; it must of necessity
possess more of prophecy than of achievement.
Katherine Cecil Thurston

With God nothing shall be impossible.
Luke 1:37

Whatever you can do or dream you can, begin it.
Boldness has genius, power, and magic in it.
Begin it now.
Johann Wolfgang von Goethe

If one advances confidently in the direction
of his dreams, and endeavors to live the life
which he has imagined, he will meet with
success unexpected in common hours.
Henry David Thoreau

A cat's eyes are windows enabling us to
see into another world.
~Irish Legend

We look into her eyes,

and we know there's more

to her than ears and nose,

fur and toes—there's the mystery

of life. Who, peering into

the eyes of living beings,

could doubt the reality

of invisible, spiritual truths?

Spiritual Nourishment

Though science has unlocked many secrets of life and nature, there remains at the core of every amazing discovery a space only God can fill. We sense it in the wonders of the universe, and we feel it in the stirrings of our own heart.

God created each of us with a physical body and a spiritual soul. We naturally wonder about God and reach out for Him because we're meant to, just as we're meant to reach out for food and eat it. Denying God's existence or His presence in our lives is as unwise as denying our need for nutritious meals. We're spiritual beings in physical bodies, because that's the way God made us!

If there's hunger and thirst in your heart...if you're reaching out for spiritual nourishment... God is there, waiting to satisfy your desire.

Grant me, dear God,
nourishment for my heart and soul.
Amen

Jesus said unto them,
I am the bread of life.
John 6:35

Are we not all divine?
Are we not all made for a higher life?
Mother Teresa

Good for the body is the work of the body,
good for the soul the work of the soul,
and good for either the work of the other.
Henry David Thoreau

In every man's heart there is an
emptiness that only God can fill.
Blaise Pascal

We are not human beings having
a spiritual experience. We are spiritual beings
having a human experience.
Pierre Teilhard de Chardin

Come to me, all you who are weary and burdened,
and I will give you rest.
Matthew 11:28 NIV

The light of God surrounds me,
The love of God enfolds me,
The power of God protects me,
The presence of God watches over me,
Where I am, God is.
Traditional Prayer

Love the animals: God has given them the
rudiments of thought and joy untroubled.
~Fyodor Dostoevsky

Anyone who watches

the ways of a cat can find

something to learn about

life and love. When we're open

to discovery, the world

around us becomes our

wise and insightful teacher.

Works in Progress

Though we may have graduated from school many years ago, we're still enrolled in the school of life. There's always something to discover and ponder, to learn and apply. At every age, we're meant to keep growing in mind and heart.

The people ahead of us in years and experience show us by their example how to navigate life's ups and downs. They have much to teach us about meeting tough challenges and enjoying simple pleasures. Those who walk along side of us give us the chance to develop friendships and close, caring relationships; and those behind us offer us opportunities to help, support, and teach.

We learn from others, and others learn from us. We're works in progress, and that's what keeps the journey so interesting and fun.

Dear God, grant me daily opportunities
to learn, help, and discover.
Amen

The one eternal lesson for us all
is how better we can love.
Henry Drummond

People seldom improve when they
have no model but themselves to copy after.
Oliver Goldsmith

Those things, which ye have both learned,
and received, and heard, and seen in me, do.
Philippians 4:9

I am defeated, and know it,
if I meet any human being from whom I find
myself unable to learn anything.
George Herbert Palmer

From the errors of others,
a wise man corrects his own.
Publilius Syrus

Very few men are wise by their own counsel,
or learned by their own teaching.
Ben Jonson

Wisdom is the principal thing;
therefore get wisdom.
Proverbs 4:7

I don't think much of a man who is not wiser today
than he was yesterday.
Abraham Lincoln

One filled with joy preaches without preaching.
Mother Teresa

Man's mind, once stretched by a new idea,
never regains its original dimensions.
Oliver Wendell Holmes

Those who'll play with cats must expect
to be scratched.
~ *Miguel de Cervantes*

The playful kitten sometimes
forgets how sharp her claws are—
ouch! But few of us will let a little
scratch keep us from enjoying her
delightful frolics. In the same way,
we won't allow minor setbacks to stop
us from pursuing worthy goals.

When Things Go Right

We've heard Murphy's Law: If anything can go wrong, it will. While the adage may exaggerate, it's no overstatement to say that any worthwhile project, goal, or objective brings its own challenges. How we meet them tests our resourcefulness and drive.

While some snags may simply slow us down a little or send us on a temporary detour, other problems may prove more formidable. Those are the kind calling for innovative ideas and new actions, and perhaps even a re-evaluation of our desired outcome. Sometimes, when what we want is not going to happen, there's something better God has in mind for us.

Yes, some things are bound to go wrong, but with God's help, you have the ingenuity, strength, and creativity to put them right.

Enable me, dear God,
to follow the right path toward my goals.
Amen

We know that all things work together for good
to them that love God.
Romans 8:28

Some minds seem almost to create themselves,
springing up under every disadvantage and
working their solitary but irresistible way
through a thousand obstacles.
Washington Irving

You cannot create experience.
You must undergo it.
Albert Camus

To be thrown upon one's own resources
is to be cast into the very lap of fortune;
for our faculties then undergo a development
and display an energy of which they
were previously unsusceptible.
Benjamin Franklin

Affliction comes to us all, not to make us sad,
but sober, not to make us sorry, but wise.
Henry Ward Beecher

If you falter in times of trouble,
how small is your strength!
Proverbs 24:10 NIV

Bad times have a scientific value.
These are occasions a good learner would not miss.
Ralph Waldo Emerson

God gives us always strength enough, and sense
enough, for everything He wants us to do.
John Ruskin

All sorts of spiritual gifts come
through privations, if they are accepted.
Janet Erskine Stuart

Puss, with delight beyond expression,
Surveyed the scene and took possession.
~William Cowper

A cat never stops to ask

permission before jumping

into his favorite chair and claiming

it for the whole afternoon.

Then why do we, instead of

gladly claiming the blessings

God sends to us, fear to take

possession of them?

Well-Blessed and Glad

Most of us can think back to a time when the door of opportunity swung open, but we hesitated at the threshold. Later we realized what a blessing the break would have been, if only we had taken advantage of it.

When God puts a blessing into our lives, He means for us to grab hold of it and use it! If He knew it was too big for us to handle, He would have offered something smaller. If He believed we shouldn't have such a wonderful gift, He would have granted it to someone else.

When God opens doors for you, He invites you to stride right on in with a heart of gratitude and humility, excitement and confidence. His gift is to you ... for you ... just because you're well-blessed you.

Dear God, enable me to possess
the opportunities You have given to me.
Amen

The opportunity that God sends
does not wake those who are asleep.
Proverb

It is at our own risk if we neglect the acquaintances and opportunities that seem to be casually
offered, and of small importance.
Amelia Huddleston Barr

I stand at the door, and knock:
if any man hear my voice, and open the door,
I will come in to him.
Revelation 3:20

When I look back now over my life and call to
mind what I might have had simply for taking
and did not take, my heart is like to break.
William Hale White

Seek ye the LORD while he may be found,
call ye upon him while he is near.
Isaiah 55:6

Opportunity is missed by most people because it is
dressed in overalls and looks like work.
Thomas Alva Edison

If a man looks sharply and attentively,
he shall see fortune.
Francis Bacon

A door that seems to stand open must
be a man's size, or it is not the door that
Providence means for him.
Henry Ward Beecher

Our opportunities to do good are our talents.
Cotton Mather

What greater gift than the love of a cat?
~*Charles Dickens*

The cat basks in the attention

of her doting human,

accepting with pure pleasure

the caresses so generously

bestowed on her. With long,

rhythmic purrs, she cherishes

the relationship that brings her so

much joy and fills her every need.

True Friends

Most of us can name many acquaintances, but only a few true friends. They're the ones who stick with us over time and are there for us through both joys and sorrows. We can count on their kindness, trust their advice, and depend on them to care, listen, and understand. Our relationship with them and theirs with us is one of mutual reward and satisfaction.

Good relationships enrich our lives in ways nothing else can. Whether we have discovered these relationships within our own family or among the people we have met along the way (or both!), each true friend gives life meaning, provides assurance and joy, and helps us grow.

To cherish good relationships—our true friends—is the surest way to keep them!

Dear God, thank You for all the
people who bless my life with love.
Amen

Greater love hath no man than this,
that a man lay down his life for his friends.
John 15:13

Friendship is the bread of the heart.
Mary Russell Mitford

To love another person is to see the face of God.
Victor Hugo

Blessed is the influence of one true,
loving human soul on another.
George Eliot

Friendship is a sheltering tree.
Samuel Taylor Coleridge

My friends are my estate.
Emily Dickinson

[Jesus said,] I have called you friends.
John 15:15

If we would build on a sure foundation
in friendship, we must love friends for their sake
rather than for our own.
Charlotte Brontë

The only way to have a friend is to be one.
Ralph Waldo Emerson

When you believe there is no love in the world,
just gaze into the eyes of the cat in your lap.
~Welsh Saying

The simple affectionate purr

of a favorite feline has the power

to renew optimism and

restore hope at the end of

a frustrating day. "Don't despair!"

is the message that often

comes without words,

but lifts the heart again.

Now What?

We had every reason to expect the best, but the worst happened. In an instant, our optimism and enthusiasm gave way to feelings of anger, frustration, confusion, and loss. "Now what?" we asked repeatedly.

In the echo of "Now what?" God's voice comes to assure us that all is not lost. Though our earnest pleadings may have been denied, God's plan and purpose for our life has been in no way diminished or thrown off-course. In fact, now that He has our undivided attention, it might be the time we'll realize what His will has been all along!

Disappointment leaves an empty space in our plans and expectations, in our hopes and dreams... a space God can fill with the assurance of His love.

Please fill, dear God, the empty spaces
in my life with the richness of Your love.
Amen

If God be for us, who can be against us?
Romans 8:31

Hope is putting faith to work
when doubting would be easier.
Author Unknown

We are troubled on every side, yet not distressed;
we are perplexed, but not in despair.
2 Corinthians 4:8

While there's life, there's hope.
Cicero

Hope, like the gleaming taper's light,
Adorns and cheers our way;
And still, as darker grows the night,
Emits a brighter ray.
Oliver Goldsmith

Hope is the thing with feathers
That perches in the soul,
And sings the tune without the words,
And never stops at all.
Emily Dickinson

Until one has loved an animal, a part of one's
soul remains unawakened.
~Anatole France

The cat, sitting in rapt attention,

is fully present to the moment.

Of her whole small, furry self,

she holds nothing back, but savors

everything to the fullest.

Like her, we're wholly alive

only when we give ourselves,

heart and soul, to the present.

Here and Now

We have a lot to think about, and so often what weighs on our mind and heart keeps us from doing anything with real love and enthusiasm. While we're at home, we're concerned about our responsibilities outside; and when we're involved in the workplace or community, we're anxious about things at home.

There comes a time when we realize we need to let go so we can embrace who we are and where we are at the moment. Leaving the house, we entrust to God our family's safety; returning home, we put behind us the issues, conflicts, and problems of the day so we can focus fully on our loved ones and friends.

Each hour, each moment, each place summons our full attention, inviting us to give of ourselves... to love wholeheartedly.

Dear God, awaken me to this moment.
Amen

No mind is much employed upon the present;
recollection and anticipation
fill up almost all our moments.
Samuel Johnson

Now is the time to be doing,
now is the time to be stirring,
now is the time to amend myself.
Thomas à Kempis

Always hold fast to the present hour.
Every state of duration, every second,
is of infinite value.
Johann Wolfgang von Goethe

The Lord is at hand.
Philippians 4:5

To those who are awake, there is one ordered
universe common to all, whereas in sleep each
person turns away from this world to one of his own.
Heraclitus

Am I a God at hand, saith the LORD,
and not a God afar off?
Jeremiah 23:23

You had better live your best and act your
best and think your best today;
for today is the sure preparation for tomorrow
and all the other tomorrows that follow.
Harriet Martineau

Our main business is not to see what lies
dimly at a distance,
but to do what lies clearly at hand.
Thomas Carlyle

A kitten is chiefly remarkable for rushing about like mad at nothing whatever, and generally stopping before it gets there.
~Agnes Repplier

On a warm and sunny afternoon,

a cat saunters through the garden

just to see what she can see.

Not everything has to have a

reason with cats— nor with her

human companions,

who often find that hard to believe.

Dilly-Dally Time

Our calendars and day planners tell the story: one appointment, activity, and meeting follows another from morning until night. Though getting out, meeting people, and seeing to our responsibilities keep us involved and purposeful, we also need appointment-free time to simply follow our whims.

A stroll taken with no destination in mind... a book picked up because you like the title... doodles drawn simply to set your imagination loose... these are aimless pastimes that, in fact, have an aim. They're a needed breather for mind and heart, moments to catch up with yourself in busy times.

And there's an added benefit. Those who allow themselves moments to dawdle are most often the ones with the energy and vitality to keep up with today's fast pace!

Dear God, enable me to let my mind
and heart relax today.
Amen

The world of reality has its limits;
the world of imagination is boundless.
Jean-Jacques Rousseau

At thy right hand there are pleasures for evermore.
Psalm 16:11

There are no rules of architecture
for a castle in the clouds.
G. K. Chesterton

Creative people are curious, flexible, persistent,
and independent with a tremendous spirit of
adventure and a love of play.
Henri Matisse

The world is but a canvas to our imaginations.
Henry David Thoreau

My heart trusted in him, and I am helped:
therefore my heart greatly rejoiceth.
Psalm 28:7

They who dream by day
are cognizant of many things
which escape those who dream only by night.
Edgar Allan Poe

To make a prairie it takes a clover and one bee,
One clover, and a bee,
And revery.
The revery alone will do
If bees are few.
Emily Dickinson

One of the most striking differences between a cat and a lie is that a cat only has nine lives.
~*Mark Twain*

A cat can wriggle through

small openings and leap across

wide gaps, and for these feats

she's said to have "nine lives."

It's a harmless bit of folklore,

unlike some of the tall tales

spun by her human companions

from time to time!

Truth Be Told

When the truth is embarrassing, or painful, or compromising, it's easy for a falsehood to slip out of our mouth. Will we be found out? Maybe, or maybe not—but a lie once told echoes within the heart for a long, long time.

Truthfulness strengthens the bonds between us. It builds trust and earns for us respect and dignity. Our commitment to the truth, even when it's uncomfortable, is a characteristic of maturity and essential for our peace of mind. Our ability to couch necessary but unflattering truths in the kindest way possible helps preserve the reputation of others, and in so doing, elevates our own.

Though the truth may humble us for a moment, it frees us to grow in honor and integrity.

Enable me, dear God,
the courage to tell the truth.
Amen

Buy the truth, and sell it not.
Proverbs 23:23

Truth is the vital breath of Beauty;
Beauty the outward form of Truth.
Grace Aguilar

We know the truth; not only by reason,
but also by the heart.
Blaise Pascal

Expedients are for the hour;
principles for the ages.
Henry Ward Beecher

There is an inmost center in us all,
where Truth abides in fullness.
Robert Browning

Truth is as impossible to be soiled
by any outward touch, as the sunbeam.
John Milton

If you seek truth, you will not seek to gain a victory
by every possible means; and when you have found
the truth, you need not fear being defeated.
Epictetus

[Jesus said,] I am the way,
the truth, and the life.
John 14:6

Care for the truth more than
what people think.
Aristotle

A kitten is the delight of a household.
All day long a comedy is played by
this incomparable actor.
~Champfleury

A kitten runs, chases, leaps,

and scampers with abandon.

Once grown, however,

he carefully guards his dignity.

Like many of his human companions,

he's quite put out should someone

happen to wound his pride.

Laugh Away

Few of us enjoy laughing at ourselves! Yet our willingness to do just that diffuses anger, deflects embarrassment, weakens offences, and turns an awkward moment for someone else into a funny joke on us.

We're more patient with the people around us when we don't take ourselves too seriously. Any affront—real or perceived—fails to evoke an insult in return, and we can listen to criticism without responding defensively. Without self-importance at stake, we can learn from what proves useful and leave the rest with a smile.

When you can laugh at yourself, you're guaranteed the first, middle, and last laugh every time!

Dear God, relieve from my attitude
the burden of self-importance.
Amen

A merry heart doeth good like a medicine.
Proverbs 17:22

Vanity is the quicksand of reason.
George Sand

A proud man is seldom a grateful man,
for he never thinks he gets as much as he deserves.
Henry Ward Beecher

Do not think of yourself more
highly than you ought.
Romans 12:3 NIV

Total absence of humor renders life impossible.
Colette

God resisteth the proud,
and giveth grace to the humble.
1 Peter 5:5

Proud people breed sad
sorrows for themselves.
Emily Brontë

The human race has one really
effective weapon, and that is laughter.
Mark Twain

Whatever you say to kittens, they always purr.
~Lewis Carroll

Of course, we could claim

that cats don't understand words,

and that's why they purr at any

lilting syllable. But maybe they

instinctively know something it

takes us years to discover:

For a happy life,

attitude is everything.

Positively Chosen

Most of us like choices. We insist on choosing our food and clothing, our music and entertainment. We gravitate to businesses that cater to our preferences, and we appreciate bosses and supervisors who offer us the flexibility we need to manage home and work responsibilities.

When it comes to harmful, undesirable feelings, however, we often forget that we have a choice here, too. When a negative thought enters our mind, we can throw it out and replace it with a positive one. When anxiety weighs down our heart, we can lighten it, if we choose, by reminding ourselves of God's presence and leaning on the strength He offers.

Your attitude is a daily choice, and it's a choice only you can make.

Grant me, dear God, the faith and courage
it takes to choose a positive attitude.
Amen

Most folks are about as happy
as they make up their minds to be.
Abraham Lincoln

Pessimism likes to build walls
where optimism builds bridges.
Author Unknown

A merry heart maketh a cheerful countenance.
Proverbs 15:13

The happiness of your life
depends upon the quality of your thoughts.
Marcus Aurelius

The greatest discovery of my generation
is that a human being can alter his life
by altering his attitude of mind.
William James

Be renewed in the spirit of your mind.
Ephesians 4:23

Great things are not something accidental,
but must certainly be willed.
Vincent van Gogh

Say you are well, or all is well with you,
And God shall hear your words
and make them true.
Ella Wheeler Wilcox

[A cat] will make itself the companion of your hours of work, of loneliness, or of sadness.
~Theophile Gautier

The quiet presence of

a cat fills a home with

a special kind of love.

God's unfailing presence

in the heart means that

we are never alone...

and always loved.

Ever-Present God

Most of us, at one time or another, have experienced loneliness. Perhaps it was after the loss of a loved one, ending of a friendship, or start of a new job in a distant city. But often in the absence of familiar faces, God's presence comes into clearer focus.

In the silence around us, He tends to our heart's deepest needs with His companionship and ever-present love. He provides us with the spiritual strength and nourishment we need to reach out to others and to move forward out of isolation and into new relationships and new experiences.

To acknowledge His presence is to find in our loneliness the one who stands ready to help and encourage, comfort and protect. It is then we realize that, no matter where we are, we are never truly alone.

> *Thank You, dear God,*
> *for Your presence in my life.*
> *Amen*

Remember never to say that you are alone,
for you are not alone;
nay, God is within.
Epictetus

He is not far from each one of us.
Acts 17:27 NIV

Are you lonely, O my brother?
Share your little with another!
Stretch a hand to one unfriended,
And your loneliness is ended.
John Oxenham

He is God in heaven above,
and in earth beneath.
Joshua 2:11

They are never alone that are
accompanied with noble thoughts.
Philip Sidney

The worst loneliness is not
to be comfortable with yourself.
Mark Twain

I believe in the sun, even when it is not shining.
I believe in love, even when I do not feel it.
I believe in God, even when He is silent.
Author Unknown

Time spent with cats is never wasted.
~*Colette*

The hours we spend stroking

a purring cat's silky coat and

admiring her jewel-toned eyes

may never make us millionaires,

but it's time well spent. The riches

gained include tranquility,

repose, and a heart accustomed

to giving and receiving love.

The Heart of Love

Our hearts are designed for love! What's more, the warmth of love is open to all of us, not just to those in a romantic relationship. Yes, God invites us to give ourselves to love, and to love generously.

God surrounds us with earth, sea, and sky… with sparkling sunlight and drifting clouds… with the sound of songbirds and the rustle of wind through trees… the fragrance of blooming flowers and zest of briny ocean swells. But how often do we stop to notice, appreciate, and love?

Love depends not on another person, but on our willingness to begin loving attentively, constantly, and joyfully. When we commit ourselves to being a loving person, the world fills with things to love.

Dear God, fill me with Your love,
so I may love!
Amen

Love is a product of habit.
Lucretius

You learn to speak by speaking,
to study by studying, to run by running,
to work by working; and just so, you learn
to love God and man by loving. Begin as a mere
apprentice and the very power of love will lead
you on to become a master of the art.
Francis de Sales

God is love.
1 John 4:8

Love should be as natural as living and breathing.
Mother Teresa

These three remain: faith, hope and love.
But the greatest of these is love.
1 Corinthians 13:13 NIV

Instead of allowing yourself to be unhappy,
just let your love grow as God wants it to grow.
Seek goodness in others. Love more persons more.
Love them more impersonally, more unselfishly,
without thought of return.
Henry Drummond

Love all of God's creation, the whole of it and
every grain of sand. Love every leaf, every ray of
God's light! Love the animals, love the plants, love
everything. If you love everything, you will soon
perceive the divine mystery in things. Once you
perceive it, you will begin to comprehend it better
every day. And you will come at last to love the
whole world with an all-embracing love.
Fyodor Dostoevsky

A kitten is so flexible that she is almost double; the hind parts are equivalent to another kitten with which the forepart plays. She does not discover that her tail belongs to her until you tread on it.
~Henry David Thoreau

Does the kitten know that

the tail she chases is her own?

But we're not unlike the playful,

frolicking kitten, because we

possess within ourselves many

more talents than we realize!

Spring Flowers and Summer Blossoms

When a subject or activity draws our interest, it's probably because we have a talent for it. And no matter where we are in life, we can find a way to bring out, nurture, and express our often long-ignored hidden talents.

There's more to each one of us than simply our job, responsibilities, or whatever we've been doing for years. When something captures our attention, it's possible a side of ourselves we've never known before is revealing itself to us. A special attraction could spark talents and skills we never knew we had, and lead to years of accomplishment, pleasure, and fulfillment.

God has blessed each one of us not with one talent, but with many. Some gifts are apparent in the springtime of life, but others, like summer blossoms, open when the time is right for them to bloom.

Help me, dear God,
discover the talents I have within me.
Amen

Let us remember that within us
there is a palace of immense magnificence.
Teresa of Avila

Men are often capable of greater things than they
perform. They are sent into the world with bills of
credit, and seldom draw to their full extent.
Horace Walpole

There are diversities of gifts,
but the same Spirit.
1 Corinthians 12:4

Enthusiasm signifies God in us.
Madame de Staël

Whosoever hath, to him shall be given,
and he shall have more abundance.
Matthew 13:12

To know what you prefer,
instead of humbly saying "Amen" to what the world
tells you you ought to prefer,
is to have kept your soul alive.
Robert Louis Stevenson

A strong passion for any object will ensure success,
for the desire of the end will point out the means.
William Hazlitt

The greatest thing in the world is to know how to
be one's own self.
Michel de Montaigne

If you shamefully misuse a cat once, she will always maintain a dignified reserve toward you afterward. You will never get her full confidence again.
~Mark Twain

Cats, just like us,

protect themselves by eyeing

warily those situations they

believe could prove dangerous.

For all of us, danger can mean

anything from physical injury to

emotional harm or discomfort.

Warning Signs

High Voltage! Deep Water! Stop Ahead! Big signs with bold letters warn us of danger. Without them, we would risk running headlong into hazards we could have avoided, if only we'd known.

So we aren't without warning, God has given us signs alerting us to spiritual danger. Clearly and without ambiguity, His Ten Commandments tell us what to stay away from for our own physical safety and emotional wellbeing. God, whose view spans past, present, and future, knows where injuries lie, no matter how harmless things may look from our point of view.

His Commandments keep us from harm, and they lead us to good ... to kindness and compassion, justice and gratitude, respect and decency, honesty and truthfulness ... and most important, a God-centered heart.

Dear God, help me to obey
Your Commandments in my life.
Amen

I will meditate in thy precepts,
and have respect unto thy ways.
Psalm 119:15

Nothing can bring you peace
but the triumph of principles.
Ralph Waldo Emerson

Be a pattern to others, and all will go well.
Cicero

The voice on conscience is so delicate
that it is easy to stifle it; but it is also so clear
that it is impossible to mistake it.
Madame de Staël

Principle is a passion for truth and right.
William Hazlitt

There is transcendent power in example.
We reform others subconsciously,
when we walk uprightly.
Anne S. Swetchine

Those who set their minds on
virtue will do no evil.
Proverb

Keep my words,
and lay up my commandments with thee.
Proverbs 7:1

When one bases life on principle,
99% of life's decisions are already made.
Author Unknown

All of the animals except for man know that the
principle business of life is to enjoy it.
~*Samuel Butler*

The cat can chase, leap,

and play without a care in

the world! Nothing weighs

on her heart, pulling her

away from life's readily

present joys.

Great Times

Many great times pass us by because we're too busy to enjoy them. Everything, from family dinners to milestone celebrations, outings with friends to kids' performances, is subject to cancellation when our calendar is crammed with other things to do.

God desires to bless us with good, memorable events, and we cancel on Him! Godly pleasure and recreation provide rest and relaxation. Celebrations, holidays, and meals with family and friends strengthen bonds and make memories to treasure long after the occasion has passed.

There's time for business...and sometimes the most important business is to put down what we're doing and embrace God's gift of a great time.

Dear God, help me choose
what's most important in my day.
Amen

To every thing there is a season, and a time to
every purpose under the heaven.
Ecclesiastes 3:1

The happiest moments of my life
have been the few which I have passed at
home in the bosom of my family.
Thomas Jefferson

What greater thing is there for two human souls
than to feel that they are joined for life...to be with
each other in silent unspeakable memories.
George Eliot

Have regular hours for work and play;
make each day both useful and pleasant,
and prove that you understand the worth
of time by employing it well.
Louisa May Alcott

Why not seize pleasure at once?
How often is happiness destroyed by preparation,
foolish preparation!
Jane Austen

Is not the life more than meat,
and the body than raiment?
Matthew 6:25

God gave us memories
that we might have roses in December.
J. M. Barrie

In the end, it's not the years in your life that count.
It's the life in your years.
Abraham Lincoln

Nothing is so difficult as to paint the cat's face.... The lines are so delicate, the eyes so strange, the movements subject to such sudden impulses, that one should be feline oneself to attempt to portray such a subject.
~Champfleury

Capturing on canvas a cat's personality is no easy task! Yet with feeling and skill, insight and diligence, the artist succeeds. When we're willing to keep on trying, who knows what masterpiece might take shape?

Go to the Finish

Many of us begin a project with high hopes of a marvelous finish. We can picture it! But soon, challenges arise, and the image of a fantastic achievement grows dimmer and dimmer.

Most often, the challenges we face on long-term projects force us to work harder than we had planned, or take more time than we meant to spend on it. Sometimes, further resources are needed, and more effort called for than we had anticipated. How we deal with these common hurdles makes the difference between stopping now—and disappointing ourselves—or meeting the challenge, and brightening up the prospect of a great outcome.

When it comes to feeling proud of the project—and of ourselves—we'll choose the challenge, and we'll go to the finish!

Grant me the determination,
dear God, to stick with worthwhile projects.
Amen

The worth of every conviction consists precisely
in the steadfastness in which it is held.
Jane Addams

Great works are performed,
not by strength, but by perseverance.
Samuel Johnson

We count them happy which endure.
James 5:11

That which we persist in doing becomes easier—
not that the nature of the task has changed, but
our ability to do it has increased.
Ralph Waldo Emerson

If you wish success in life,
make perseverance your bosom friend.
Joseph Addison

Be strong in the Lord,
and in the power of his might.
Ephesians 6:10

It is necessary to try to surpass one's self always;
this occupation ought to last as long as life.
Christina Augusta

The block of granite which was an obstacle in the
pathway of the weak becomes a stepping stone in
the pathway of the strong.
Thomas Carlyle

One can go a long way after one is tired.
Proverb

Do you see that kitten chasing so prettily her own tail? If you could look with her eyes, you might see her surrounded with hundreds of figures performing complex dramas, with tragic and comic issues, long conversations, many characters, many ups and downs of fate.
~Ralph Waldo Emerson

Anyone who enjoys the company of cats knows that no two are alike. Each has his and her own ways and routines, whimsies and imaginings. Each whiskered companion fills a special place in someone's life, just like each of us.

A Place for You

There's no one quite like you. You play a part in your family's memories and loved ones' favorite moments. Your skills and talents impress others, and many have been inspired and encouraged by the things you do and say.

When you're out and about, your smile warms hearts and leaves people feeling good about themselves. The many kindnesses you do—most without even realizing you're doing anything special—leave a trail of generosity paid forward time and time again. More than you know, your thoughtfulness has made all the difference in someone's day.

If you've ever wondered if there's a place for you, just look around. There are people—who can count the number?—who are glad that God created you just the way you are.

Thank You, God,
for where I am and who I am.
Amen

I will praise thee;
for I am fearfully and wonderfully made.
Psalm 139:14

If God had wanted me otherwise,
He would have created me otherwise.
Johann Wolfgang von Goethe

The great and glorious masterpiece of man is to
know how to live to purpose.
Michel de Montaigne

It is the chiefest point of happiness that a man is
willing to be what he is.
Erasmus

That kind of life is most happy which affords us
most opportunities of gaining our own esteem.
Samuel Johnson

[The LORD said,]
"Before I formed you in the womb I knew you."
Jeremiah 1:5 NIV

A man cannot be comfortable
without his own approval.
Mark Twain

How can we send the highest love
to others if we do not have it for ourselves?
Prentice Mulford

When I play with my cat, who knows
whether she is not amusing herself with
me more than I with her.
~Michel de Montaigne

We entertain our cats

(and exercise them, too)

when we dangle their favorite

toy in front of them, or roll a

ball for them to chase across

the room. And we can't help

but feel happy, because the happiness

we give always returns to us.

Generous Giving, Grateful Receiving

If we want to make a difference, we give. The time and attention we provide to those who depend on us enhances their wellbeing and shows them how much they are loved. In return, we receive the satisfaction of giving, and often in a way no one else could. There are other important kinds of giving, too.

Donations to organizations we support go toward feeding the hungry, providing for children in distressed circumstances, sheltering animals in need, advancing medical research, and more. In return, we get back the satisfaction of knowing that without our support, these causes would be less effective.

As givers, we can graciously and gratefully receive help from others. After all, we know well the blessings that come with being able to give.

Dear God, enable me to generously
give and gratefully receive.
Amen

It is in giving oneself that one receives.
Francis of Assisi

God loveth a cheerful giver.
2 Corinthians 9:7

We should give as we would receive, cheerfully,
quickly, and without hesitation; for there is no
grace in a gift that sticks to the fingers.
Seneca

When I give, I give myself.
Walt Whitman

She gives most who gives with joy.
Mother Teresa

[Jesus said,] Freely ye have received, freely give.
Matthew 10:8

God looks not to the quantity of the gift,
but to the quality of the givers.
Francis Quarles

He which soweth bountifully
shall reap also bountifully.
2 Corinthians 9:6

We enjoy thoroughly only the
pleasure that we give.
Alexandre Dumas

Cats are mysterious kind of folk. There is more passing in their minds than we are aware of.
~Sir Walter Scott

The cat is described by the color

of his eyes and his fur, his size,

and his distinctive markings.

Yet invisible at first glance is

his affectionate personality,

love for his home, and devotion

to his human companion.

Just like him, we're more

than outward appearance alone.

Look Again

Our appearance tells something about who we are, but falls far short of telling the whole story. From simply how we look, others aren't able to discern our true character, our dreams, and our deepest thoughts. The things most of us hold most dear—high values, special memories, cherished beliefs, prized accomplishments—are invisible to others' eyes.

And the same is true for everyone we meet. We cannot know the joys and sorrows inside each heart merely by looking at hair, skin, and clothes; we'll never learn what others can teach us if we dismiss them based on size and shape alone. It's the heart that counts, and the heart we discover by accepting, listening, and understanding.

Appearance is like the first hello—a mere introduction to what's most important.

Help me, dear God,
to avoid judging anyone based on appearance.
Amen

Judge not according to the appearance.
John 7:24

How little do they see what really is, who frame
their hasty judgments upon that which seems.
Robert Southey

Fashion is the science of appearance,
and it inspires one with the desire to seem
rather than to be.
Henry Fielding

Be kind, for everyone you meet
is fighting a hard battle.
Author Unknown

All that glitters is not gold.
Miguel de Cervantes

Beware, so long as you live,
of judging men by their outward appearance.
Jean de La Fontaine

Things do not pass for what they are,
but for what they seem.
Most things are judged by their jackets.
Baltasar Gracian

God does not judge by external appearance.
Galatians 2:6 NIV

The bosom can ache beneath
diamond brooches; and many a blithe heart
dances under coarse wool.
Edwin Hubbel Chapin

We should be careful to get out of an experience only the wisdom that is in it, and stop there; lest we be like the cat that sits down on a hot stove lid. She will never sit down on a hot stove lid again, and that is well; but also she will never sit down on a cold one anymore.

~Mark Twain

If something frightens her,

a cat will avoid the place;

but her human companions,

after careful evaluation of the facts,

will return, conquering their fear

with the wisdom they have earned.

Another Go

We're heart-broken in a relationship…in the workplace…in the trust we gave to a person or an organization. For some, being let down once convinces us to withhold our love, loyalty, or trust rather than risk another letdown. For others, disillusionment results in an objective look at what went wrong and why; and then another go, though this time with wisdom and experience we didn't have before.

Objectivity isn't easy when we're disappointed or discouraged. Our emotions tend to amplify what went wrong, even to the point of unnecessarily blaming ourselves or others. Often it takes a conscious effort on our part to step back so we can look at the facts. The advice of supportive and knowledgeable friends can help.

God is there, too. He cares deeply about broken hearts.

Dear God, enable me to see
with an objective eye.
Amen

No passion so effectively robs the mind of all its
powers of acting and reasoning as fear.
Edmund Burke

He healeth the broken in heart,
and bindeth up their wounds.
Psalm 147:3

Wisdom is oftentimes nearer when
we stoop than when we soar.
William Wordsworth

Our bravest and best lessons are not learned
through success, but through misadventure.
Amos Bronson Alcott

[God] giveth wisdom unto the wise,
and knowledge to them that know understanding.
Daniel 2:21

The art of being wise is the art
of knowing what to overlook.
William James

Do the thing you fear most
and the death of fear is certain.
Mark Twain

Apparent failure may hold in its rough shell
the germs of a success that will blossom in time,
and bear fruit throughout eternity.
Frances Ellen Watkins Harper

Watch a cat when it enters a room for the first time. It searches and smells about, it is not quiet for a moment, it trusts nothing until it has examined and made acquaintance with everything.

~Jean-Jacques Rousseau

"Look before you leap"

is an adage practiced by the cat,

for she'll use all her powers of

perception before venturing

into unfamiliar places.

We would do well to

follow her example!

Foundation Building

Good preparation is the foundation of successful projects. The information we gather before launching into a new venture helps us avoid common beginners' mistakes, and knowing what to expect keeps us from being blindsided by ordinary frustrations. The questions we pose and the answers we discover help ensure a good outcome.

Whether we're considering a different job or new hobby, an exotic vacation or advanced degree, preparation boosts our knowledge, builds our confidence, and increases our readiness for any opportunities that may come. When we talk to people already where we'd like to be, we not only learn from their experience and insight, but make connections that may work to our advantage later on.

Lay the foundation, and then build with well-founded faith and confidence!

> *Dear God, grant me the patience*
> *and wisdom to prepare.*
> *Amen*

Chance favors the prepared mind.
Louis Pasteur

Be prepared in season and out of season.
2 Timothy 4:2 NIV

I will study and get ready
and then maybe the chance will come.
Abraham Lincoln

What had seemed easy in imagination
was rather hard in reality.
L. M. Montgomery

Prepare your minds for action.
1 Peter 1:13 NIV

A bad beginning makes a bad ending.
Euripides

The man who is prepared
has his battle half-fought.
Miguel de Cervantes

What we prepare for is what we shall get.
William Graham Sumner

Nothing is as deflating as a cat's
perfect indifference.
~Author Unknown

A cat carries her head high,

regardless of what's being said

about her. Who wouldn't admire

her natural dignity? By contrast,

her human companions

sometimes cringe in fear of the

critical remark, the opposing voice.

Speak Up, Speak Out

Speaking out is risky. As soon as the words leave our mouth, they're examined and analyzed. Perhaps others will judge us harshly for holding an unpopular view, or maybe our reputation will suffer once our thoughts are known. But when something truly matters, isn't it worth the risk?

Sometimes, to stand up for ourselves and what we know is right, we're obliged to speak out, regardless of what others may think or say. When the topic matters, we're remiss if we don't make our thoughts known. Even if others disagree, or even criticize us, we know we've done the right thing by speaking from the heart.

Fear of judgment pales in comparison with the strength of mind and character gained when we stand up for godly principles and values.

Grant me the courage, dear God,
to defend what's right.
Amen

Risk anything! Care no more for the opinion of others, for those voices. Do the hardest thing on earth for you. Act for yourself. Face the truth.
Katherine Mansfield

Silence is not always tact
and it is tact that is golden, not silence.
Samuel Butler

To dare is to lose one's footing momentarily.
To not dare is to lose oneself.
Søren Kierkegaard

Lord, behold their threatenings:
and grant unto thy servants, that with all
boldness they may speak thy word.
Acts 4:29

I believe in getting into hot water;
it keeps you clean.
G. K. Chesterton

Speak ye every man the truth to his neighbour.
Zechariah 8:16

To avoid an occasion for our virtues
is a worse degree of failure than to push
forward pluckily and make a fall.
Robert Louis Stevenson

Many great ideas have been lost because the people
who had them could not stand being laughed at.
Author Unknown

I dip my pen in the blackest ink,
because I'm not afraid of falling into my inkpot.
Ralph Waldo Emerson

'Tis for her own good that the cat purrs.
~Irish Saying

What pure bliss she

signals in the soft, velvety rumble

of her contented purr!

Whoever can proclaim

with the cat, "I am content!"

possesses rare wealth,

and that person, even though

penniless, will never be poor.

A Contented Heart

We would find it hard to spend even a day free of advertisements for goods and services. That's why it's important for us not so much to avoid them, but to turn them to our advantage. Indeed, many ads inform us of things that will ease our workload, bring us pleasure, and enhance our health and wellbeing.

But if we allow things pitched to us, or purchased by our neighbor, to take away contentment, we're headed for trouble. We'll soon discover that things in themselves—no matter how much we're able to acquire—never bring satisfaction. There always will be something else, and something else after that.

A contented heart is a choice, and when we choose this possession above all others, we find we have everything we'll ever need—and more.

Dear God, help me choose contentment
over anything else.
Amen

When a man is contented with himself
and his resources, all is well.
William Hazlitt

Perfect bliss grows only
in the heart made tranquil.
Proverb

Economy, prudence, and a simple life
are the sure masters of need, and will often
accomplish that which their opposites,
with a fortune at hand, will fail to do.
Clara Barton

I have learned, in whatsoever state I am,
therewith to be content.
Philippians 4:11

Contentment is not the fulfillment
of what you want, but the realization of
how much you already have.
Author Unknown

Godliness with contentment is great gain.
1 Timothy 6:6

You never know what is enough
unless you know what is more than enough.
William Blake

No man can be poor that has enough,
nor rich, that covets more than he has.
Seneca

Wedging itself between face and book,
the cat's expression says, "You didn't
really want to read that, did you?"
~Author Unknown

The cat's doting companion

lets him get by with whatever

he wants. Why? Because a

cat is a cat! And anyway,

to not always insist on getting

our own way is a generous,

unselfish way to live.

Unselfishness in Action

Have you ever opted for a friend's plans instead of your own? Of course you have! And while you may have thoroughly enjoyed the activity, no doubt part of your pleasure rested with knowing how happy you made your friend. It's a nice compliment you're giving someone when you agree, "Yes, let's do it your way!"

Not always demanding our own way shows others that we care enough about them to listen to, and go along with, their good suggestions and ideas. Our willingness to substitute another's proposal for our own is a sign of unselfishness, as well as a kind and generous gesture.

There's another benefit to saying "Yes" to others: Next time, it's likely they will be eager to go along with what we would like to do!

Grant me the willingness, dear God,
to not demand my own way.
Amen

Do nothing out of selfish ambition
or vain conceit, but in humility consider
others better than yourselves.
Philippians 2:3 NIV

Ignorance is the mother of presumption.
Marie de Gournay

A wise unselfishness is not a surrender
of yourself to the wishes of anyone, but only to
the best discoverable course of action.
David Seabury

Kindness is a golden chain
by which society is bound together.
Johann Wolfgang von Goethe

Real unselfishness consists in sharing
the interests of others.
George Santayana

We can really respect a man only if he doesn't
always look out for himself
Johann Wolfgang von Goethe

Keep back thy servant also from presumptuous
sins; let them not have dominion over me.
Psalm 19:13

For having lived long, I have experienced
many instances of being obliged, by better
information or fuller consideration, to change
opinions, even on important subjects, which I
once thought right but found to be otherwise.
Benjamin Franklin

To cultivate kindness is a
valuable part of the business of life.
Samuel Johnson

When she walked … she stretched out long and thin like a little tiger, and held her head high to look over the grass as if she were treading the jungle.

~Sarah Orne Jewett

A healthy kitten strides

through the house with all

the confidence of a queen

in her castle. Even though small,

fragile, and delicate, the kitten

compares herself to no one,

for she is proud to be herself.

Pride That Counts

We might say, "There's pride … and there's pride." The wrong kind of pride fills us with a sense of entitlement and self-importance; but when we take godly pride in ourselves, we possess dignity and self-respect.

God has made each of us not with indifference, but with infinite love. So we can take pride in ourselves and in who we are, He invites us to come to Him when our wrongs drag us down and our mistakes make self-esteem impossible. In our sorrow, God reminds us of His Son Jesus, who earned for us complete forgiveness.

It's because of Jesus that you can walk with your head held high … with dignity … with all the right kind of pride, because God has lovingly created you.

Dear God, create in me
godly pride in the person I am.
Amen

Create in me a clean heart, O God;
and renew a right spirit within me.
Psalm 51:10

It is difficult to make a man miserable while he
feels he is worthy of himself and claims kindred to
the great God who made him.
Abraham Lincoln

He that respects himself is safe from others;
he wears a coat of mail that none can pierce.
Henry Wadsworth Longfellow

I have no right, by anything I do or say, to demean
a human being in his own eyes. What matters is
not what I think of him; it is what he thinks of
himself. To undermine a man's self-respect is a sin.
Antoine de Saint-Exupery

We must never undervalue any person.
Francis de Sales

Never esteem anything as of advantage
to you that will make you break your word
or lose your self-respect.
Marcus Aurelius

If we confess our sins,
he is faithful and just to forgive us our sins,
and to cleanse us from all unrighteousness.
1 John 1:9

He who undervalues himself
is justly undervalued by others.
William Hazlitt

Animals are such agreeable friends—they ask no questions, they pass no criticisms.
~George Eliot

No matter how difficult the day has been, cats and dogs welcome us back home with unqualified delight. They have no interest in judging us, because they know what's really important.

Heart of Compassion

We know we're with a true friend when we can reveal the inmost thoughts of our heart, confident we will not be judged. The friend will not think less of us because of what we're saying, but will listen with compassion and understanding.

One of the nicest gifts we can give others is to be that friend—the one who chooses empathy over opinion … concern over disapproval … connection over separation. After all, there's little anyone can tell us that we cannot, in some way, identify with, for all of us have had feelings and experiences that have brought us shame. It is not for us to guess how we would have responded, given our friend's perspective, choices, and circumstances.

We judge rightly when we remember that it's compassion and understanding we most desire from others.

Pour compassion into my heart, dear God,
because You are compassionate.
Amen

How seldom we weigh our neighbor
in the same balance with ourselves.
Thomas à Kempis

The caustic which you handle in order to scorch
others may happen to sear your own fingers.
George Eliot

Judge not, and ye shall not be judged.
Luke 6:37

You can't depend on your judgment
when your imagination is out of focus.
Mark Twain

When you judge people,
you have no time to love them.
Mother Teresa

In the same way you judge others,
you will be judged, and with the measure you use,
it will be measured to you.
Matthew 7:2 NIV

We are all wise when we admonish others,
and yet we know not when we trip ourselves.
Euripides

Judging others makes us blind,
whereas love is illuminating.
Dietrich Bonhoeffer

Any fool can criticize,
condemn and complain, and most fools do.
Benjamin Franklin

There are no ordinary cats.
~Colette

Though the two gray tabbies

look alike to strangers,

their affectionate companion

sees their subtle, distinct markings

and knows their individual voices.

In the same way, no two days

are alike for those willing to

discover the unique blessings

each has to offer.

What's New?

"So, what's new?" someone asks. And you know what the most common answer is: "Not much."

Though the person who casually asks "What's new?" isn't looking for a detailed answer, it's a question we can ask ourselves each morning, and answer it with a list. If we do, we'll realize that there's plenty new. The day itself is ripe for discovery and experience. It has never been before, and will never be again. Our thoughts are today built on all that has gone before, and today will shape them further, deepening and expanding them as we open ourselves to what's around us.

When we look around with eyes full of excitement for all life has to offer, we're going to find that the only answer to "What's new?" is: "Everything!"

Dear God, help me appreciate
the wonder of each new day.
Amen

Cause me to hear thy lovingkindness
in the morning; for in thee do I trust.
Psalm 143:8

No matter what looms ahead, if you can eat today,
enjoy today, mix good cheer with friends today,
enjoy it and bless God for it.
Henry Ward Beecher

There is nothing that cannot happen today.
Mark Twain

We must learn to reawaken
and keep ourselves awake, not by mechanical aids,
but by an infinite expectation of the dawn.
Henry David Thoreau

There's no such thing as an ordinary day to those
who see it in an extraordinary way.
Saying

"Old times" never come back and I suppose it's
just as well. What comes back is a new morning
every day in the year, and that's better.
George E. Woodberry

It is never too late to be
what you might have been.
George Eliot

Don't count the day—make the days count.
Author Unknown

There is no more intrepid explorer
than a kitten.
~Champfleury

Cats are curious creatures,

and it's through their curiosity

that they learn about the world

around them. We, too, learn about

the world (and ourselves)

when we ask questions,

probe for clues, and never settle

for easy, unexamined thinking.

Peeling Back the Layers

Being curious is like peeling an onion: the more layers you peel away, you uncover even more layers until you finally get to the center of the bulb. Similarly, significant truths are often buried beneath layers of false assumptions, deliberate smokescreens, or as yet undiscovered facts.

Following our curiosity takes effort. Like a persistent detective, we may need to follow several leads before we can reach a satisfactory conclusion. Curiosity also comes with a certain amount of risk when we're attempting to expose or prove wrongdoing. For these reasons, being curious about meaningful subjects isn't for the hesitant or faint-of-heart!

Your relationship to God is something well deserving of your curiosity. At its core, you'll find the heart of the God who calls you by name, and loves you dearly.

Lead me to You, dear God.
Amen

Instinct is the nose of the mind.
Delphine de Girardin

It is the nature, and the advantage, of strong
people that they can bring out the crucial questions and form a clear opinion about them.
Dietrich Bonhoeffer

Better to ask twice than to lose your way once.
Proverb

The greatest virtue of man is perhaps curiosity.
Anatole France

Curiosity is one of the most permanent and certain
characteristics of a vigorous intellect.
Samuel Johnson

Be ye stedfast, unmovable,
always abounding in the work of the Lord.
1 Corinthians 15:58

A sudden bold and unexpected question doth
many times surprise a man and lay him open.
Francis Bacon

Curiosity is lying in wait for every secret.
Ralph Waldo Emerson

Everything that moves serves to interest
and amuse a cat.
~*Francois-Augustin de Paradis de Moncrif*

A dangling string...

leaves skittering across the lawn...

the play of light and shadow

on the wall will keep a cat at

rapt attention! There's no need

for high-priced gadgets for

those who know the pleasure

of joyful, simple living.

Simple Living

What does it mean to live simply? For some, it requires moving to a rustic cabin deep in the woods, far from the complexities of modern-day life. Yet there's another equally valid definition, and that's separating what is meaningful, functional, and beautiful in our life from the trivial, useless, and unnecessary.

Simple living means discarding unneeded possessions—those things that, if we didn't have them, we would scarcely miss them. Without them, our home would be less cluttered, more easily managed, and the hours spent maintaining them free for other things. In the same way, simple living allows us to say "no" to activities that sound tempting, but truly do not fit into our desire for a freer, less busy schedule.

The joy of living can begin today, right where you are.

Dear God,
show me where I can simplify my life.
Amen

'Tis the gift to be simple,
'Tis the gift to be free...
Shaker Hymm

The average man is apt to attempt
more than he can accomplish, to seek to
acquire more than he needs and to exhaust
himself in senseless competition.
Alice Hegan Rice

I am bound to praise the simple life,
because I have lived it and found it good.
John Burroughs

Simplicity is the ultimate sophistication.
Leonardo da Vinci

Life itself can be very simple;
it is we who insist on making it complicated.
Author Unknown

Have nothing in your houses that you do not know
to be useful or believe to be beautiful.
William Morris

Simplicity, simplicity, simplicity!
I say let your affairs be as one, two, three
and not a hundred or a thousand.
Henry David Thoreau

The only simplicity that matters
is the simplicity of the heart.
G. K. Chesterton

[A cat] will lie the whole evening on your knee, purring and happy in your society.
~Theophile Gautier

What bliss for a cat who

gets to spend quiet hours in

the company of her loving human

companion! She seeks no one else,

for she knows she has everything

she needs right where she is.

The Company We Keep

Most of us have seen this more than once: A person is standing surrounded by his friends, yet busily calling or texting someone else, and barely listening to the voices within earshot!

While our electronic devices and social networks are great tools for us to keep in touch with one another, our primary concern remains with the people actually around us. They are the ones speaking to us about their successes, concerns, and joys...the ones whose voices, faces, and gestures can tell us more than a long-distance message could ever reveal. It's their heart that our attentive response can lift up and encourage, inspire and support. It's their shoulder we can touch, their hand we can hold.

Our message means the most to the company we're keeping now.

Thank You, dear God,
for those who are present in my life today.
Amen

Ah, how good it feels!
The hand of an old friend.
Henry Wadsworth Longfellow

Friends are those rare people who ask how you
are and then wait for the answer.
Author Unknown

If we walk in the light, as he is in the light,
we have fellowship one with another.
1 John 1:7

My idea of good company is the company
of clever, well-informed people who
have a great deal of conversation;
that is what I call good company.
Jane Austen

I have friends in overalls whose friendship I would
not swap for the favor of the kings of the world.
Thomas Alva Edison

Iron sharpeneth iron; so a man sharpeneth
the countenance of his friend.
Proverbs 27:17

"Stay" is a charming word in a friend's vocabulary.
Louisa May Alcott

The most I can do for my friend
is simply be his friend.
Henry David Thoreau

A little drowsing cat is an image of a perfect beatitude.
~*Champfleury*

The cat closes her eyes

in calm repose. No fearful heart

for her, because she knows

she's protected and cared for,

supported and loved by

someone who cherishes her.

God's Delight

If there is or has been a beloved cat in your life, you know the pleasure of caring for a little being completely dependent on you. You do everything you can to show her your love. You soothe her when she's frightened, stroke her when she comes to you for rubs, and tend to her physical and emotional health. There's nothing about her that you don't care about.

Even greater than any one of us could care for another living being, however, is God's care for each of us. He comforts us in our distresses... He responds to us when we call on Him... He provides for our physical, emotional, and spiritual needs. And on top of everything, He delights in us!

God longs to touch you with His all-encompassing love. You belong to Him, and He takes delight in you.

Dear God, keep me securely in Your care!
Amen

He careth for you.
1 Peter 5:7